How

D0823711

Learn How to Tie a Tie In 6 Easy Steps

by

Robert Seiffert

Table of Contents

Introduction

Whether you are looking for a new necktie knot to express your personal style, or just need to learn how to tie an easy knot in a hurry, this guide can help you.

Keep in mind that for the best appearance, you want to choose a knot which goes with the width and material of the tie while at the same time complementing the shirt's collar shape.

Nine popular knots are described below, along with photographs of the steps involved (each knot only requires 6 steps).

Don't be surprised if your first attempts at a new knot don't turn out perfectly. They all take a bit of practice, but rest assured that you will soon be able to tie each one quickly and professionally.

Here's to your tie success!

Robert Seiffert

The Knots

(Before you get started, please note that all of the tying directions are given as seen facing the wearer.)

Half Windsor

This is a very popular knot, and is a fun alternative to the Windsor. This knot works best with medium weight ties and also shorter ties. Wear it with any dress shirt.

The following pages illustrate steps 1 through 6.

1. Place the wide end to the left in front of the narrow end.

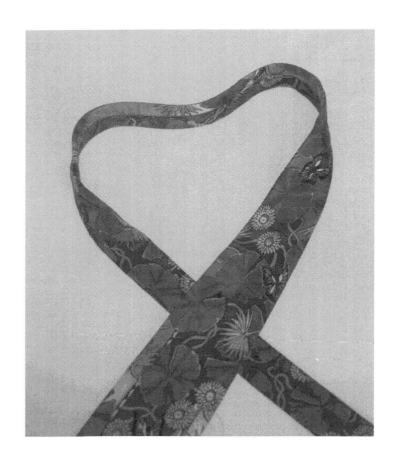

2. Wrap the wide end behind and upwards through the neck loop.

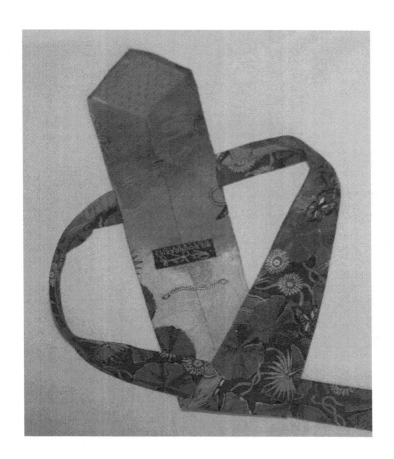

3. Now bring the wide end over the neck loop to the left, then to the right behind where the knot is forming (so that the back side shows).

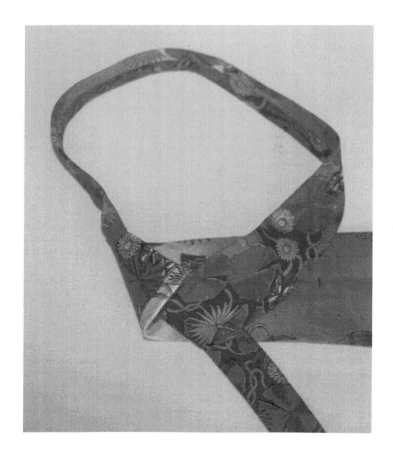

4. Wrap the wide end again to the left over the narrow end where the knot is forming.

5. Bring the wide end once more behind and upwards through the neck loop.

6. Tuck the wide end through the front loop. Tighten the knot and slip it into shape at the collar.

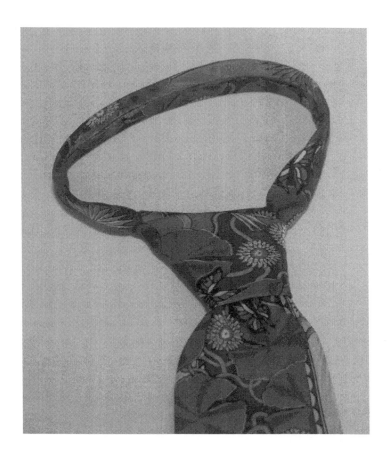

Windsor

This is a classic knot, and much of the appeal is due to its beautiful symmetry which is achieved by the double wrapping around the neck loop. It is a bit more difficult to tie than the Half Windsor, and works best with spread collar shirts.

The following pages illustrate steps 1 through 6.

1. Cross the wide end over the narrow end to the left and bring it from behind to the front, and then up and through the neck loop.

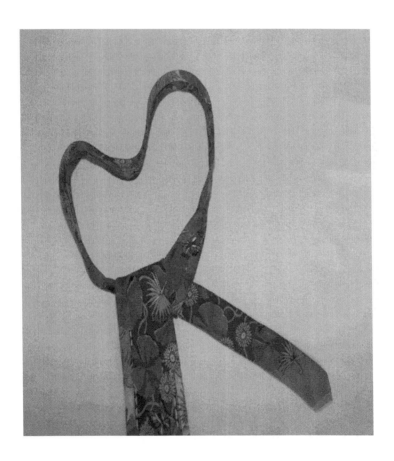

2. Pull the wide end down and wrap it behind to the right.

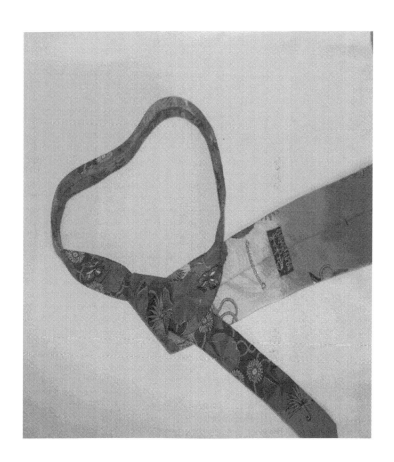

3. Now wrap the wide end up, in front, and over the neck loop, where the knot is forming, so that the back side shows and extends to the left.

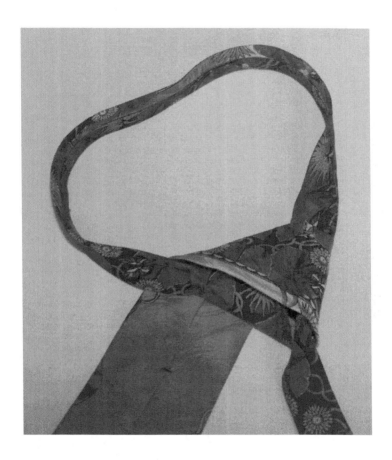

4. Loop the wide end horizontally and to the right, in front of the knot which is being created.

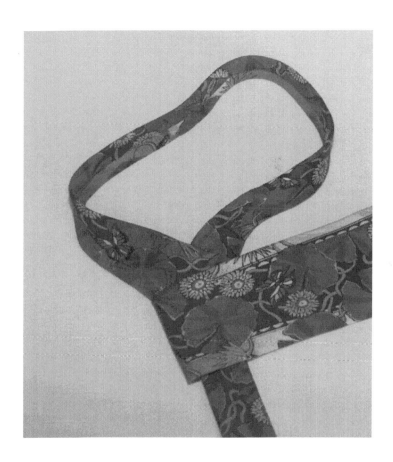

5. Now bring the wide end from behind, up through the neck loop.

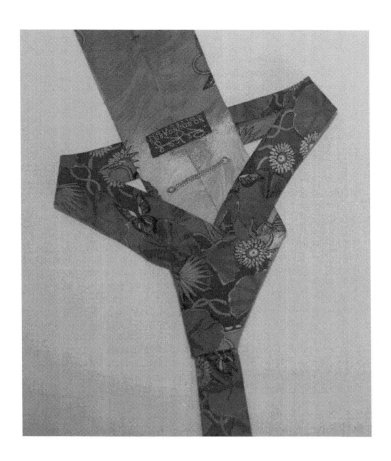

6. Tuck the wide end through the front loop that was just formed. Tighten and shape the knot.

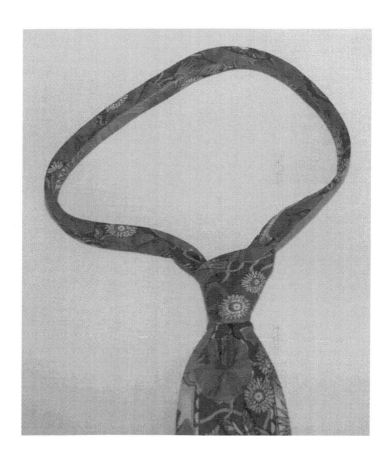

Freestyle

This knot combines elements of the Simple knot and the Windsor. Due to its bulkiness, using a medium-weight silk tie works best. Often worn with a spread collar shirt.

The following pages illustrate steps 1 through 6.

1. Cross the ends so that the wide end runs to the left on top of the narrow end.

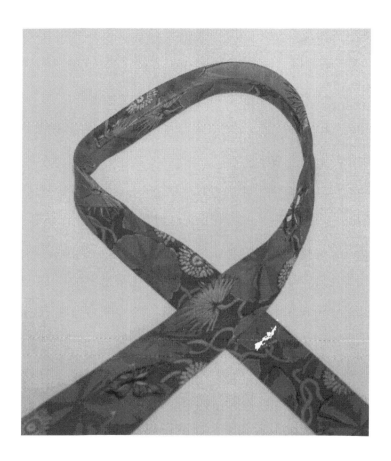

2. Wrap the wide end behind the narrow end horizontally to the right, and fold it up in front of and then through the neck loop to the left, so that the back seam shows.

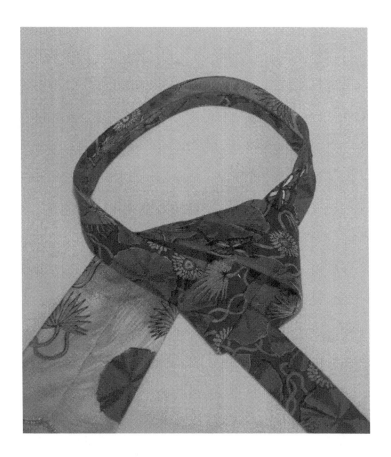

3. Wrap the wide end horizontally back to the right.

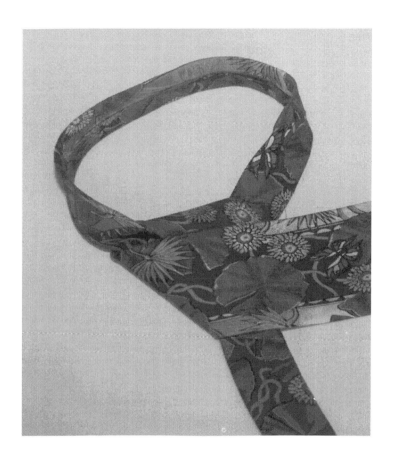

4. Bring the wide end through the neck loop.

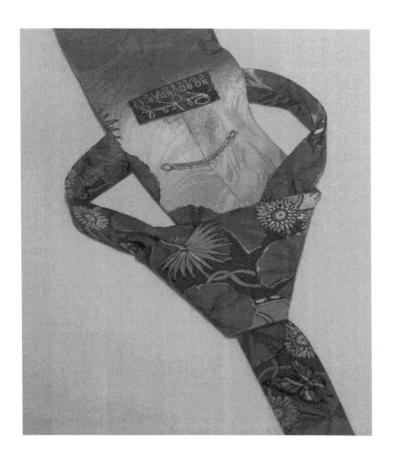

5. Tuck the wide end down through the front loop.

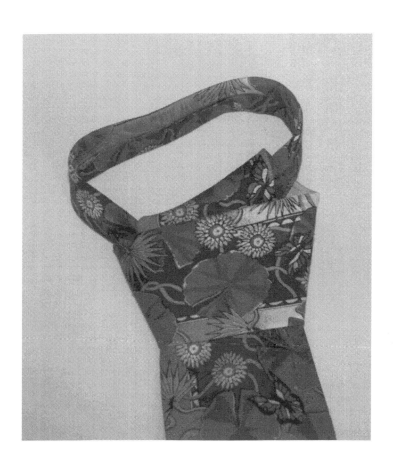

6. Draw the knot tight and shape it as desired.

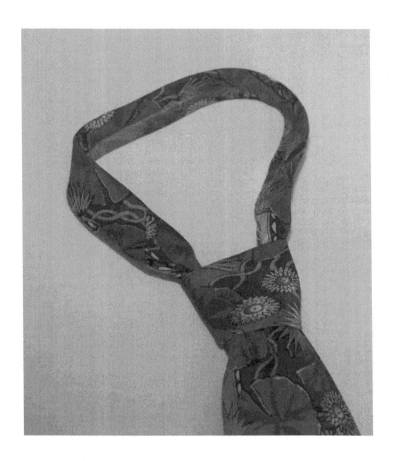

Simple Knot

Also known as "Four in Hand", this is a very popular knot for beginners because it is easy to tie. Slightly asymmetrical, it works well with silk or wool tie fabrics, and is typically used with button-down dress shirts.

The following pages illustrate steps 1 through 6.

1. Cross the ends so that the wide end lies over the narrow end and points to the left.

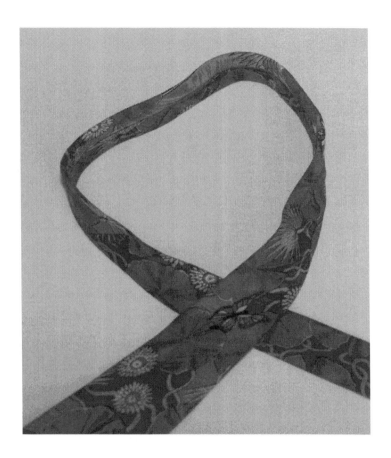

2. Bring the wide end behind the narrow end horizontally to the right.

3. Wrap the wide end in front of the narrow end, where the knot is forming.

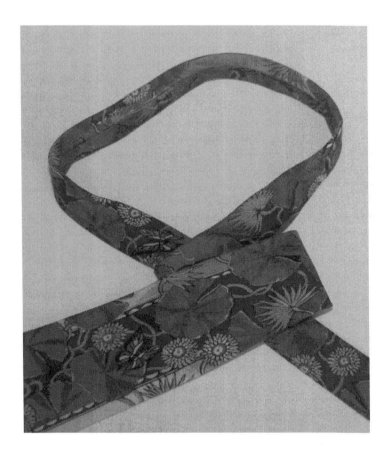

4. Pull the wide end behind and upwards through the neck loop.

5. Tuck the wide end down through the front loop.

6. Tighten the knot and adjust the shape.

Double Knot

As you might expect, this knot uses double wrapping, and is best suited to narrow and somewhat longer ties made of a light fabric. Typically worn with spread collar shirts.

The following pages illustrate steps 1 through 6.

1. Cross the ends so that the wide end goes over the narrow end and points to the left.

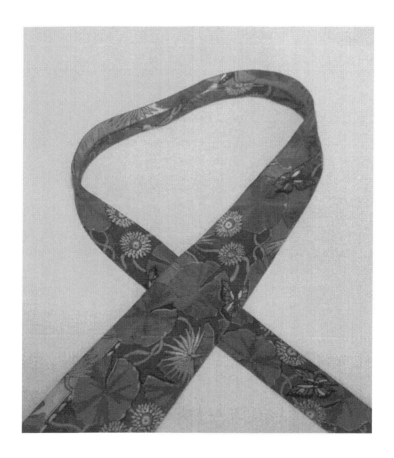

2. Wrap the wide end around the narrow end so that it crosses in front again and points horizontally to the left.

3. Wrap the wide end again around the narrow end, pointing to the right.

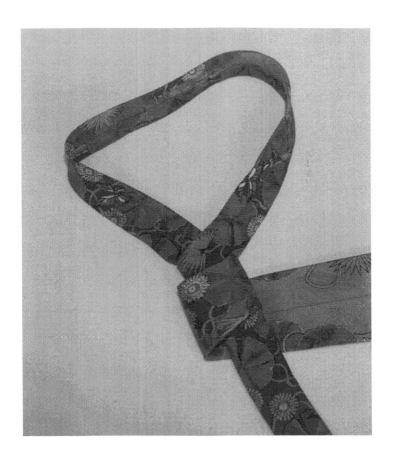

4. Bring the wide end back over the front so that it points to the left again.

5. Bring the wide end behind and up through the neck loop.

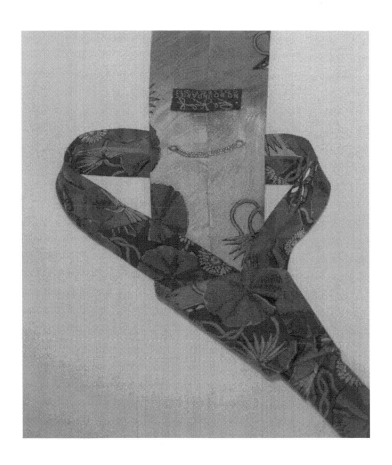

6. Tuck the wide end down through the front loop of the double wrapping. Tighten the knot and shape it so that the double wrapping is visible.

Cross Knot

This stylish and somewhat unusual knot is moderately difficult to tie, and works best with lighter fabrics. Use this knot with any dress shirt.

The following pages illustrate steps 1 through 6.

1. Cross the ends with the smooth side facing out. The wide end lies above the narrow one at first, pointing to the left. Then it is wrapped behind the narrow end so that it points to the right with the seam facing out.

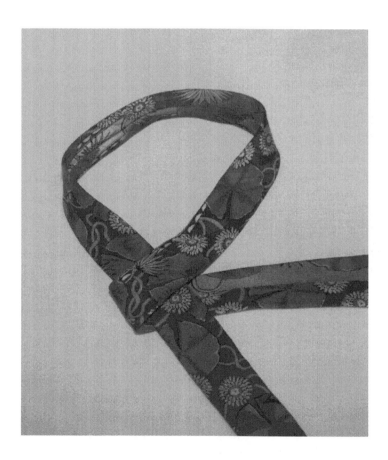

2. Fold the wide end up and through the neck loop so that it points to the left with the seam facing out.

3. Wrap the wide end completely around the narrow end so that it points to the left again.

4. Fold the wide end to the right again and pull it up through the neck loop.

5. Bring the wide end down through the front loop of the double wrap.

6. Draw the knot tight, ensuring that the double wrapping is visible.

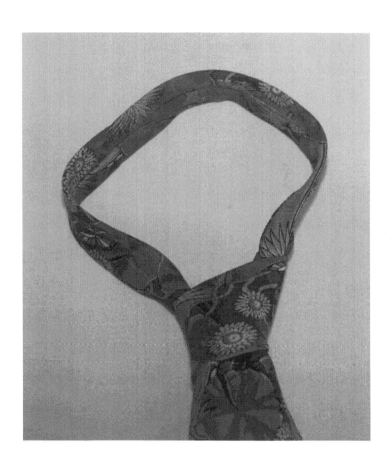

Shelby

Also known as "Pratt" or "The American", this knot is best suited for shorter ties with a thick lining. It looks somewhat similar to the Windsor, and should be worn with spread collar shirts.

The following pages illustrate steps 1 through 6.

1. Cross the ends with the back seams facing out. The narrow end lies above the wide end and points to the right.

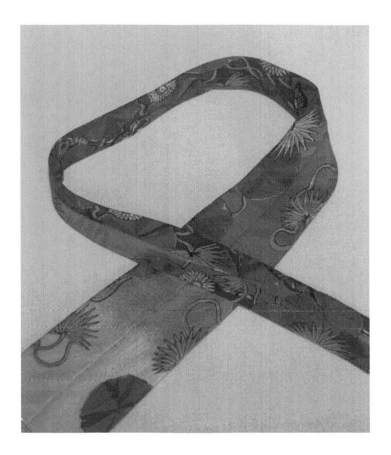

2. Bring the wide end forward, up, and over the neck loop. Pull it down with the back seam still showing.

3. Draw the wrapping tight.

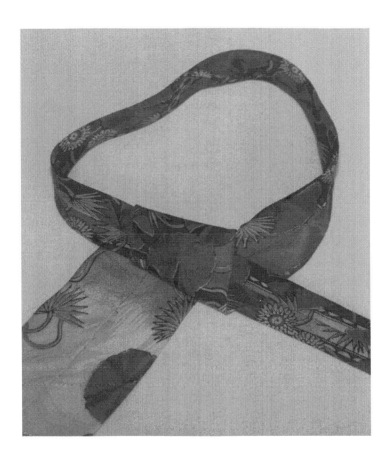

4. Fold the wide end horizontally from left to right over the narrow end.

5. Bring the wide end up again through the neck loop.

6. Tuck the wide end down through the front loop and draw the knot tight.

New Classic

This is a somewhat narrow knot and works best with light to medium-weight ties that are not too long. Use with any dress shirt.

The following pages illustrate steps 1 through 6.

1. Cross the ends with the back seam facing out. The narrow end lies above the wide end and points to the right.

2. Bring the wide end up so that the smooth side faces out.

3. Pull the wide end through the neck loop horizontally to the right.

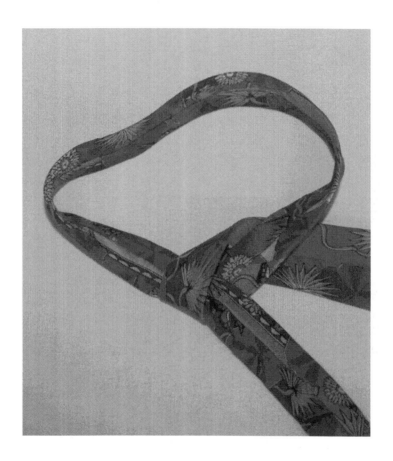

4. Wrap the wide end back over the narrow end horizontally to the left.

5. Bring the wide end from behind up through the neck loop and tuck it through the front loop.

6. Draw the knot tight and shape it to the collar.

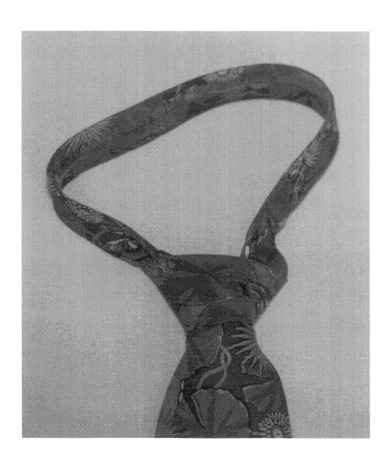

Diagonal Knot

This is an unusual design and really draws the eye with its diagonal knot. It works well with subdued patterns, but is very difficult to tie. Looks great with an unbuttoned dress shirt.

The following pages illustrate steps 1 through 6.

1. Cross the ends so that the wide end lies above the narrow end and points to the left, with the smooth sides facing out.

2. Wrap the wide end beneath the narrow end so that it points to the right with the seam facing out.

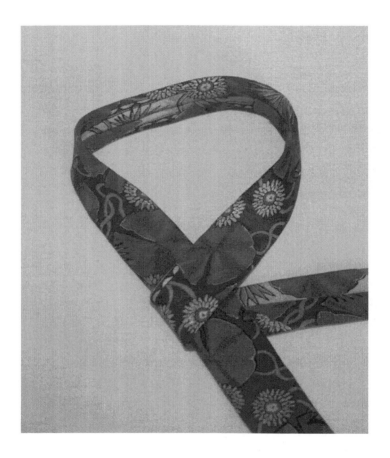

3. Wrap the wide end once completely around the narrow end so that it points to the right again.

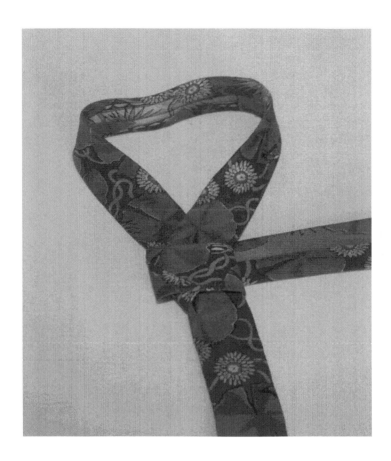

4. Bring the wide end from the front up through the neck loop so that it points to the left with the seam facing out.

5. Tuck the wide end down through the front loop.

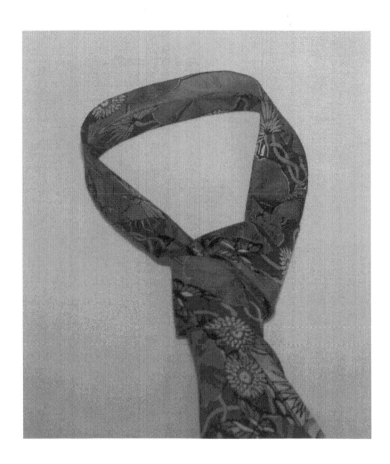

6. Draw the knot tight as you push it upward and shape it.

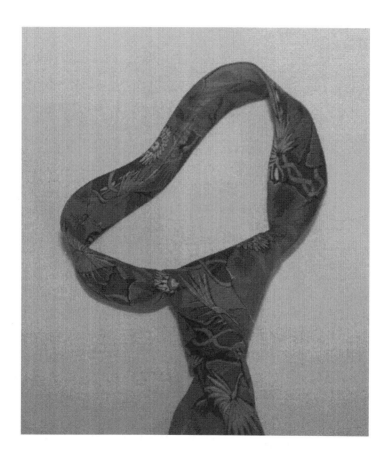